A HISTORY OF THE

Medieval Church

AND THE

Bible

LIVING HISTORY THREADS

A History of the Medieval Church and the Bible

ISBN 978-0-9816569-5-3

Author: Esther Bean

Photo credits: Aiwaz.net: 14a, 15, 17; Bethel College/Mennonite Library and Archives: 11; ©istockphoto.com/AlterYourReality: 30a; Wikimedia Commons/ Creative Commons: Tilman2007/iii, Nicolas Sanchez/4, Ricardo André Frantz/5a, Tango7174/5c, Sicarr/6, Bbruno/9, David Ball/20a,30b, Shakko/20c.

Cover design: Kyle Brubaker

Cover picture: *Eton College* painted by Canaletto

Living History Threads is a history curriculum developed by Faith Builders Resource Group. For more information about Living History Threads, email fbresource@fbep.org or phone 877-222-4769.

Distributed by:
Christian Learning Resource
28500 Guys Mills Road
Guys Mills, PA 16327
www.christianlearning.org
877-222-4769

A HISTORY OF THE

Medieval Church

AND THE

Bible

Name:

School:

Grade: _three_

A HISTORY OF THE

Medieval Church

When you think of the Medieval Times in Europe, what comes to your mind?

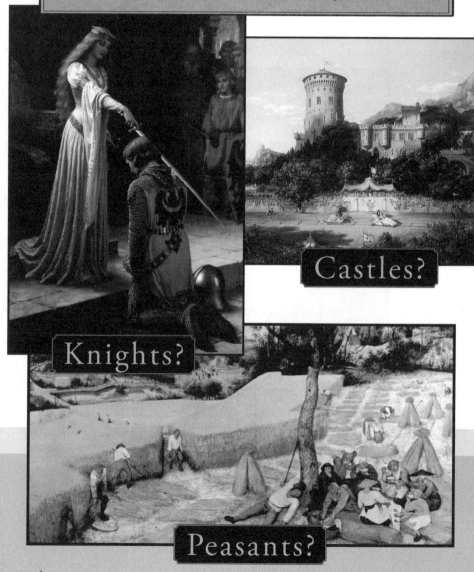

Castles?

Knights?

Peasants?

Cathedrals?

Crusades?

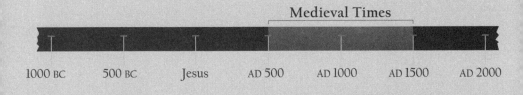

The Medieval Times refers to about AD 500–1500.

Medieval Times

| 1000 BC | 500 BC | Jesus | AD 500 | AD 1000 | AD 1500 | AD 2000 |

● Notre Dame Cathedral

● Lincoln Cathedral

● Mary Queen of the World Cathedral-Basilica

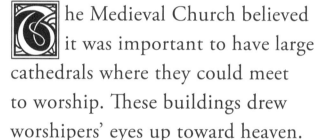

The Medieval Church believed it was important to have large cathedrals where they could meet to worship. These buildings drew worshipers' eyes up toward heaven.

Few people could afford to be well educated. Those who were rich were taught to read and could study the Bible. However, if a poor boy had outstanding ability, he could live at a monastery and learn to read and write.

Notre Dame Cathedral in Paris, France

There are five people you should know who are important in the history of the Medieval Church.

St. Patrick was a missionary to the Irish. He grew up in a very wealthy family in Britain, but as a young man he was captured by Irish raiders and forced to work as a slave in Ireland. After returning to his family, Patrick sensed God's call to move back to Ireland, this time as a missionary.

Patrick was a missionary in Ireland for twenty-nine years. It is believed that he baptized over 120,000 Irishmen and started at least three hundred churches.

One folk tale says Patrick drove the snakes from Ireland. Maybe this story started because snakes are often associated with Satan, and Patrick tried very hard to drive away an idol-worshiping cult.

Patrick wrote a prayer about how Christ is always with us.

Christ with me, Christ before me,
Christ behind me, Christ in me!
Christ below me, Christ above me.
Christ at my right, Christ at my left!
Christ in breadth, Christ in length,
Christ in height!
Christ in the heart of
everyone who thinks of me,
Christ in the mouth of
everyone who speaks to me,
Christ in every eye that sees me,
Christ in every ear that hears me!

Peter Valdes (or Waldo) was an extremely rich merchant in France. He had become rich by cheating people when he loaned them money. Peter had everything he wanted, but he did not have peace with God. He wondered, "How can I have peace?" Someone told him Jesus' words to the rich young ruler, "If you would be perfect, sell all you have, give it to the poor, and come follow Me."

Peter obeyed. He gave his wife a choice: she could have either all of his personal goods or all of his lands. When she chose the lands, Peter sold his belongings. He paid back the people he had cheated, and hired well-educated men to translate the Bible into

French. He gave the rest of the money to the poor.

Peter noticed that many of the Catholic Church leaders were more interested in making money than in teaching people what was right. Peter and his followers did not like this greediness. Instead, they tried to be poor. They became known as the Poor Men of Lyons.

Peter and his Poor Men wanted to stay in the Catholic Church, but they had many disagreements with church leaders. The church leaders did not want the Poor Men to preach without permission from their bishops, but even when they were refused permission, the Poor Men traveled around

preaching openly. The Church thought the Poor Men should be punished for disobeying their bishops.

Peter Valdes died in 1217. His followers became known as the Waldensians. The Catholic Church hated them. They were hunted and chased. The children of Waldensians were taken away from them and put into orphanages. Some of Peter's followers were sent away as galley slaves. Thousands were tortured and killed. Some Waldensians tried to hide in caves. Their persecutors lit fires at the cave entrances to kill the Waldensians by smothering them with smoke.

Waldensians depicted as witches

Although many Waldensians were killed, some escaped. There are Waldensians living today in northern Italy and France.

Burning of about eighty
Waldensians at Strasbourg

Bernard of Clairvaux (1090–1153)

ernard of Clairvaux was one of the most influential church leaders of his time. He founded a monastery that became so popular that about one hundred other monasteries also became associated with him and his teachings.

Bernard is known for his many writings, such as letters, books, and essays. On the next page is a poem he wrote about Jesus' death. Have you ever sung this song?

Bernard of Clairvaux is also remembered for strongly promoting the Second Crusade to the Holy Lands. Bernard spoke powerfully and convinced many people that God wanted the

Christians to fight the Muslims. He was extremely disappointed when the Crusade was a disaster.

O sacred Head, now wounded, with grief and shame weighed down,
Now scornfully surrounded with thorns, Thine only crown;
How pale Thou art with anguish, with sore abuse and scorn!
How does that visage languish, which once was bright as morn!

What language shall I borrow to thank Thee, dearest friend,
For this Thy dying sorrow, Thy pity without end?
O make me Thine forever, and should I fainting be,
Lord, let me never, never outlive my love to Thee.

St. Francis of Assisi has been nicknamed "Preacher to the Birds." It is said that when he preached, the birds were silent and listened to him. He chose to live a poor life and instructed his followers to do the same. He visited the sultan in Egypt to try to persuade him to become a Christian. Francis is remembered for his gentleness and goodness. You may have heard or sung his famous peace prayer.

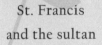

St. Francis
and the sultan

Lord, make me
an instrument of your peace.

Where there is hatred,
Let me sow love;
Where there is injury, pardon;
Where there is doubt, faith;
Where there is despair, hope;
Where there is darkness, light;
And where there is sadness, joy.

O Divine Master, grant that I may
Not so much seek to be consoled
As to console;
To be understood
As to understand;
To be loved as to love.
For it is in giving that we receive;
It is in pardoning that we are
pardoned.
And it is in dying that we are
Born to eternal life.

Amen

Thomas Aquinas is remembered for his remarkable thinking abilities. He studied and wrote much about belief in God and the teachings of Jesus. Thomas Aquinas was the leading church scholar of the Medieval Church times.

Because Thomas was a big, quiet man, he was nicknamed "The Dumb Ox." However, one of his teachers recognized his intelligence and said, "This is an ox whose braying all Europe will hear."

His teacher was correct. Thomas Aquinas tried to organize beliefs about God to prove that He exists and to show what He and His creation are like.

O Creator past all telling,

You have appointed from the treasures of Your wisdom

the hierarchies of angels,

disposing them in wondrous order

above the bright heavens,

and have so beautifully set out all parts of the universe.

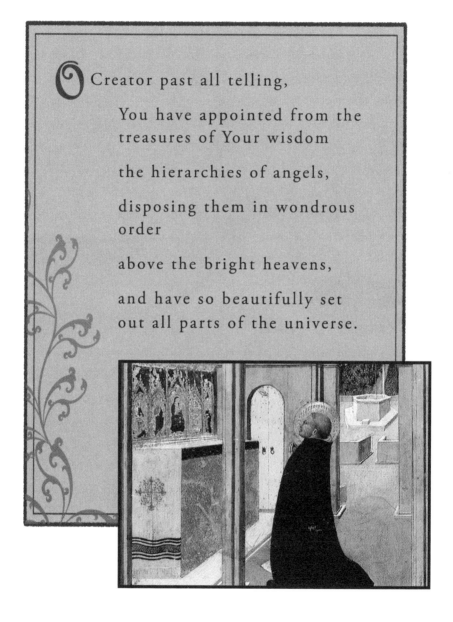

A HISTORY OF THE

Bible

● 1859 Family Bible

● Psalm 21

● Jeweled Bible Cover

ow many Bibles do you have in your house? One? Ten? Twenty?

In the Medieval Times there were few Bibles. Only very wealthy people and churches could afford one. Bibles were expensive because they had to

be copied by hand. Monks painstakingly lettered and decorated beautiful copies of the

Scriptures on parchment. Sometimes the pages and covers were decorated with gold or jewels.

Originally, the Old Testament had been written in Hebrew, and the New Testament in Greek. However, during the Medieval Times, Latin Bibles were used. That was how the Catholic Church said it must be done. Only educated people could read Latin, and no one spoke it as their own language.

People wanted to be able to read and understand the Bible. Certain men tackled the huge project of translating the Bible into the languages of their people.

Not everyone was happy about this plan. The church leaders tried to stop these men and burn all the "heretical" books they could find. Still, these translators persevered in the face of great danger.

John Wycliffe (1320–1384)

The higher the hill, the stronger the wind: so the loftier the life, the stronger the enemy's temptations.

John Wycliffe faced many trials as he tried to translate the Bible into English. The English of his time would sound strange to us, because language keeps changing. When he translated, Wycliffe used English that his hearers could understand.

Burning Wycliffe's body

22

John Wycliffe was the first person to produce handwritten copies of the complete Bible in English. Wycliffe was declared a heretic. However, people so highly respected him that he could not be convicted in a trial. He wrote and preached until he died. But Wycliffe's enemies hated him so much that forty-one years after he died, they dug up his body and burned it. Many people read his translation or heard about him after his death and believed that the Bible should be in their language too. Wycliffe was a leader in Bible translations.

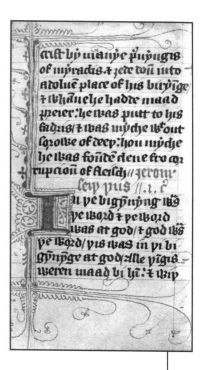

Beginning of John 1
from Wycliffe's
Bible, 1410

Truth conquers.

Jan Hus is remembered for promoting truth—truth at all costs. He said,

> **I** would not, for a chapel full of gold, recede from the truth.

Jan Hus was from Bohemia, which is now the Czech Republic. He had read John Wycliffe's writings and wanted the Bible to be translated into the Czech language.

Jan Hus boldly rebuked church leaders for their wealth and for their false teachings.

Bethlehem Chapel in Prague

At the Bethlehem Chapel in Prague, he hung pictures contrasting Jesus' disciples and the present church leaders. This made the church leaders furious.

The Church Council said they wanted to discuss Jan's beliefs with him. They promised safety, but when Jan arrived, the Council threw him into prison. Jan Hus was condemned and burned for his beliefs. When the fire had been lit, Jan sang a prayer.

Execution of
Jan Hus

Johannes Gutenberg (1400–1468)

Johannes Gutenberg did not translate the Bible. However, he made it possible for many copies of the Bible to be printed. He is credited with inventing the first printing press with movable type. This press could print many books in a short time, which made them much less expensive. The first book Johannes printed was the Bible. Now even people who were not wealthy could afford Bibles.

A print shop in 1568

Religious truth is captive in a small number of little manuscripts which guard the common treasures, instead of expanding them.

Let us break the seal which binds these holy things;

let us give wings to truth that it may fly with the Word, no longer prepared at vast expense, but multitudes everlastingly by a machine which never wearies to every soul which enters life.

Beginning of the Gutenberg Bible

Johannes Gutenberg

In England it was still against the law to read an English Bible. However, William Tyndale took the risk of translating the Bible into English. He translated from the original languages, Hebrew and Greek. This made his translation more accurate than Wycliffe's translation from Latin about 150 years before.

When a priest taunted Tyndale about his translation, Tyndale replied, "If God spare my life, ere many years, I will cause the boy who drives the plow to know more of the Scriptures than thou."

William Tyndale had to escape for his life many times. He lived in other countries that he hoped were safer than England. When his Bible translation was printed, copies were smuggled into England and distributed secretly. Even so, the church authorities burned many copies.

One of Tyndale's former friends betrayed him to the church leaders. His last words before he died were, "Lord, open the king of England's eyes."

A page from
Tyndale's Bible
(1536)

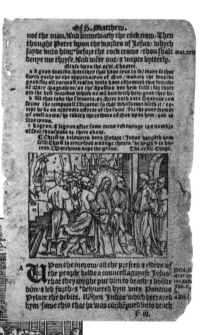

Tyndale's
execution

"Lord opē the King of Englands eies."

The next time you look at a Bible, think about the many people who have read God's words and tried to follow them. Thank God for those who have worked hard and suffered much so that you can have the Bible in your own language. Pray for Bible translators today who are helping more people to have the Bible in their own language.

Thank God for giving you the precious gift of His Word. Maybe you can give a Bible to someone who does not have one.